WILD WATER

Swimming in the Wild

BY S.L. HAMILTON

A&D Xtreme
An imprint of Abdo Publishing | www.abdopublishing.com

Visit us at
www.abdopublishing.com

Published by Abdo Publishing Company, a division of ABDO, PO Box 398166, Minneapolis, Minnesota 55439. Copyright ©2016 by Abdo Consulting Group, Inc. International copyrights reserved in all countries. No part of this book may be reproduced in any form without written permission from the publisher. A&D Xtreme™ is a trademark and logo of Abdo Publishing Company.

Printed in the United States of America, North Mankato, Minnesota.
052015
092015

Editor: John Hamilton
Graphic Design: Sue Hamilton
Cover Design: Sue Hamilton
Cover Photo: Alamy
Interior Photos: Alamy-pgs 8-9 & 12-13;
AP-pgs 1, 2-3, 10-11 & 16-17; Corbis-pgs 4-5,
7, 14-15, 18-19 & 30-31; Glow Images-pgs 20-29;
Granger-pg 6; iStock-pg 32.

Websites
To learn more about Wild Water action, visit booklinks. abdopublishing.com. These links are routinely monitored and updated to provide the most current information available.

Library of Congress Control Number: 2015930945

Cataloging-in-Publication Data

Hamilton, S.L.
 Swimming in the wild / S.L. Hamilton.
   p. cm. -- (Wild water)
ISBN 978-1-62403-752-8
1. Swimming--Juvenile literature.   2. Marine animals--Juvenile literature.
I. Title.
797.21--dc23
                                        2015930945

Contents

Swimming in the Wild

Marine mammals and fish are a source of beauty and enjoyment in our seas and oceans. Many of these creatures are known for their curiosity and friendliness towards people. Humans love swimming with them.

XTREME QUOTE – *"They are curious about us, but not the way we're fascinated about them."* –*Tori Cullins, marine biologist, on dolphins*

History

Stories of people swimming with sea creatures can be traced to ancient times. A Greek myth tells of a musician named Arion. Both people and animals loved Arion's wonderful playing. While at sea, sailors tried to kill Arion to steal his riches. Arion jumped overboard to escape. A dolphin, drawn to the ship by the music, carried Arion safely back to land.

A boy and dolphin playing together.

People have been drawn to sea creatures for thousands of years. In 109 AD, Roman senator Pliny the Younger penned one of the first written accounts of a boy and dolphin team. The boy and a dolphin named Simo performed tricks for delighted visitors to the town of Hippo, on the coast of northern Africa.

Dolphins

Wild dolphins are often drawn to people in the water. These curious marine mammals are also known to swim near moving boats. "Wake-riding" dolphins swim up to 18 miles per hour (30 kph). They have fun, and boaters get a safe close encounter with them.

XTREME FACT – Dolphins can become aggressive. Although wild dolphins can swim away when they no longer want to interact with people, these predators have been known to push people underwater or inflict serious bites. Dolphins may also be hurt or killed when humans defend themselves. It is safer to enjoy wild dolphins from a distance, from a boat, or from shore.

Captive dolphins have contact with humans every day. Swimming with them in a pool is considered safer than swimming with wild dolphins. However, even captive dolphins are big marine mammals. They may weigh from 330 to 1,430 pounds (150 to 649 kg). It's important to follow the rules to stay safe.

A girl enjoys swimming with a dolphin at Discovery Cove in Orlando, Florida.

XTREME FACT – Bottlenose dolphins have the largest brain-to-body-mass size of any mammal on Earth.

Many people believe that swimming with dolphins helps them feel better. This is called "dolphin therapy." People of all ages enjoy working on their treatments or exercises together with these amazing marine mammals.

Whales

A sperm whale may weigh 35 to 45 tons (32 to 41 metric tons). Females and calves usually swim in protective "pods" of 15 to 20 animals. Males swim alone or roam from pod to pod. Sperm whales are often shy around people. Some freedivers, people who do not use scuba gear, are able to swim with the great marine mammals.

XTREME FACT – *Swimming with sperm whales is risky. A sperm whale is able to swallow a person whole. They are more likely to hit a swimmer with their massive tail or paralyze a human with their incredibly loud echolocation sounds. They are the loudest animals on Earth, with clicks so intense the sounds can injure people. Sperm whales are best viewed from a distance.*

Humpback whales are called "gentle giants." They weigh as much as 30 to 40 tons (27 to 36 metric tons). Even though they are huge, humpbacks are very aware of people in the water with them.

Humpbacks try to avoid hitting swimmers with their huge tail flukes or pectoral fins. Humpback whale calves often approach delighted swimmers, viewing people with great curiosity.

XTREME FACT – For safety, it is best if people swim with humpback whales near the water's surface. Many people also view them from a distance in boats or ships.

Sharks

Sharks are powerful predators. Swimming with them is frightening and fun. Most people swim with sharks in a tour group. The group includes experienced divers who keep watch for any unusual or threatening movements by the fish.

Most sharks are not interested in eating humans unless they feel threatened. To say it is "safe" to swim with them is questionable. Many people prefer to go into the water in a shark-proof cage. It is an amazing experience to watch sharks in their natural habitat.

A freediver swims with a tiger shark in West End, Bahamas.

XTREME QUOTE – "Don't shark dive in murky water, don't shark dive alone, and don't act like prey, or they will treat you like prey."   —Andy Casagrande IV, shark cinematographer

Shark populations are declining due to overfishing. It's important that sharks aren't harmed simply because people want to swim close to the great predators. However, sharks are naturally curious. While divers should try to keep a safe distance, a shark may still swim up to you!

A juvenile hammerhead shark checks out a diver.

Whale sharks are the biggest shark and the biggest fish in the sea. These giants can grow up to 46 feet (14 m) long and weigh up to 15 tons (14 metric tons). They are often found close to coastlines and near the water's surface. Since they mostly pay little attention to people, swimming with whale sharks is common.

XTREME FACT – The "whale" in a whale shark's name refers to its huge size. It is not a whale. It is a fish.

Rays

Manta rays are popular with swimmers in the wild. Most rays have a long, whip-like tail, armed with a poisonous spine. A manta ray has a shorter tail and no dangerous stinger.

XTREME FACT - Manta rays have no teeth. They feed their giant, 3,000-pound (1,361-kg) bodies by filtering plankton, small fish, and crustaceans into their mouths while they swim.

Manta rays are the largest species of ray, with a wingspan reaching 22 feet (7 m). They have two flaps that extend in front of their eyes. These "cephalic lobes" are used to push food into their mouths as they swim. People love watching these smooth-moving cousins to the shark.

A diver encounters a beautiful, but dangerous, spotted eagle ray.

Some people accidentally encounter or choose to swim with dangerous stingrays or electric rays. These fish are equipped to protect themselves. Some have whip-like tails that can tear open flesh and deliver a dose of poison. Some have hard, bony spines that stab their victims. Electric rays send out shocks of up to 200 volts that stun both prey and predator. It is best for swimmers to leave when these rays appear.

XTREME FACT - Wildlife expert and TV personality Steve Irwin was killed in 2006 by a huge, 8-foot (2.4-m) bull ray (stingray) while filming a show entitled "Ocean's Deadliest."

Sea Turtles

Green sea turtles weigh up to 700 pounds (318 kg). These big marine reptiles usually do not mind sharing the water with swimmers. If they want to escape, their large flippers can propel them away at speeds of up to 35 miles per hour (56 kph).

Green sea turtles are endangered. To protect them, people must never touch or ride them. If a turtle shows signs of stress (yawning, head bobbing, or flipper swipes over the forehead), it's time to swim away.

Jellyfish

Most jellyfish have stinging tentacles that cause intense pain. People should stay away from them. However, that is not true of the jellyfish on the island country of Palau. Its Jellyfish Lake holds golden and moon jellyfish that are not harmful to people. Swimmers can join millions of these jellies in the water and be amazed at their beauty.

XTREME FACT - *Jellyfish Lake was cut off from the sea about 12,000 years ago. Since there were no natural predators, the jellyfish evolved into today's unique species without stingers.*

Glossary

AGGRESSIVE
Likely to attack with, or without, a reason
to do so.

CRUSTACEAN
An animal with a hard shell and many jointed
legs. Shrimp, crabs, lobsters, and crayfish are
crustaceans.

ECHOLOCATION
The ability of certain animals, such as bats
or dolphins, to find food or other objects by
sending out sound waves and listening to the
echoes that bounce back. A type of natural sonar.

ENDANGERED
An animal or plant with so few
living that it is in danger of dying
out and being gone from the Earth.

FLUKE
Either side of a dolphin's or
whale's tail, which meet in a "v"
in the middle. The flukes move
up and down to propel the animals
through the water.

FREEDIVER
A person who holds their breath and dives underwater for up to several minutes. Freedivers do not use oxygen tanks.

MARINE BIOLOGIST
A person who studies animal and plant life in saltwater environments, such as oceans and seas.

MARINE MAMMALS
Saltwater mammals that breathe air and give birth to live young, such as dolphins, seals, and whales.

PECTORAL FINS
Fins found on either side of a fish or marine mammal's body.

PLANKTON
Tiny or microscopic organisms that float or drift in huge numbers in both freshwater and saltwater.

POD
A group of marine mammals that live together.

PREDATOR
An animal or fish that feeds on other animals or fish.

SCUBA
Scuba stands for "self-contained underwater breathing apparatus." It is a device that allows divers to breathe underwater for a certain period of time.

Index